S0-BOL-588

FANTASTIC SPORTS FACTS

# BASEBALL

Michael Hurley

Raintree

Chicago, Illinois

© 2013 Raintree
an imprint of Capstone Global Library, LLC
Chicago, Illinois

To contact Capstone Global Library please phone 800-747-4992, or visit our website www.capstonepub.com

Edited by Catherine Veitch, Sian Smith, and John-Paul Wilkins
Designed by Richard Parker
Picture research by Tracy Cummins
Originated by Capstone Global Library Ltd
Printed and bound in China

16  15  14  13  12
10 9 8 7 6 5 4 3 2 1

**Library of Congress Cataloging-in-Publication Data**
Cataloging-in-Publication data is available at the Library of Congress.
ISBN 978-1-4109-5107-6 (hbk)
ISBN 978-1-4109-5114-4 (pbk)

**Acknowledgments**
The author and publisher are grateful to the following for permission to reproduce copyright material: Flickr p. 13 (Dale Bryant); Getty Images pp. 6 (Lloyd Fox/Baltimore Sun/MCT), 7 (Christian Petersen), 8 (National Baseball Hall of Fame Library/MLB Photos), 17 (Transcendental Graphics), 18 (Stephen Dunn), 21 right (Mitchell Layton/Getty Images), 22 (Jim Rogash), 24 (Tony Tomsic/MLB Photos), 25 (Mark Cunningham/MLB Photos), 26 (Allan Grant//Time Life Pictures); Newscom pp. 5 (EPA/JACK SMITH), 9 (JP5\ZOB/WENN), 10, 11, 16 (ZUMA Press), 12 (UPI Photo/Hector Mata), 14 (Jim McIsaac/Newsday/MCT), 20 right (PM SportsChrome), 23 (Cindy Yamanaka/ZUMA Press), 27 (TSN/Icon SMI); Shutterstock pp. 4 (© JustASC), 15 left (© zentilia), 15 right (© Kevin Hill Illustration), 19 (© Thomas Barrat), 20 left (© Danny Smythe), 21 left (© ILYA AKINSHIN).

Cover photograph of Ichiro Suzuki of the Seattle Mariners batting against the Oakland Athletics at Safeco Field on August 1, 2011 in Seattle, Washington, reproduced with permission of Getty Images (Otto Greule Jr), and a baseball reproduced with permission of Shutterstock (mexrix).

Every effort has been made to contact copyright holders of any material reproduced in this book. Any omissions will be rectified in subsequent printings if notice is given to the publisher.

All the Internet addresses (URLs) given in this book were valid at the time of going to press. However, due to the dynamic nature of the Internet, some addresses may have changed, or sites may have changed or ceased to exist since publication. While the author and publisher regret any inconvenience this may cause readers, no responsibility for any such changes can be accepted by either the author or the publisher.

# Contents

Some words are printed in bold, **like this**. You can find out what they mean by looking in the glossary.

# Baseball Basics

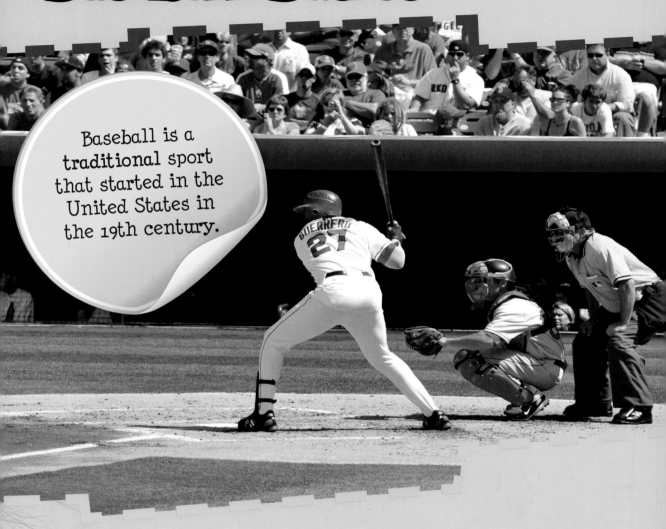

Baseball is a traditional sport that started in the United States in the 19th century.

The top baseball league in the world is Major League Baseball (MLB). It is based in the United States. There is also a very popular baseball league in Japan.

4

## DID YOU KNOW?

The Japanese league is known as Nippon Professional Baseball (NPB).

The World Baseball Classic is a tournament that teams from around the world play in.

5

# Record Runs

When the Texas Rangers beat the Baltimore Orioles in 2007, they set a modern record for the biggest **winning margin**. They won 30–3.

Incredibly, the Orioles had taken a 3-0 lead at the start of the game!

Rangers batsman Ramon Vazquez hit two **home runs** in the game.

## FUN FACT

The highest total of runs scored in an MLB game is 49. The Chicago Cubs beat the Philadelphia Phillies 26-23 in 1922.

7

# Giant Bats

The bat used by **legendary** player Babe Ruth (right in picture below) was the largest ever used in baseball. It did not stop him from hitting over 700 **home runs**!

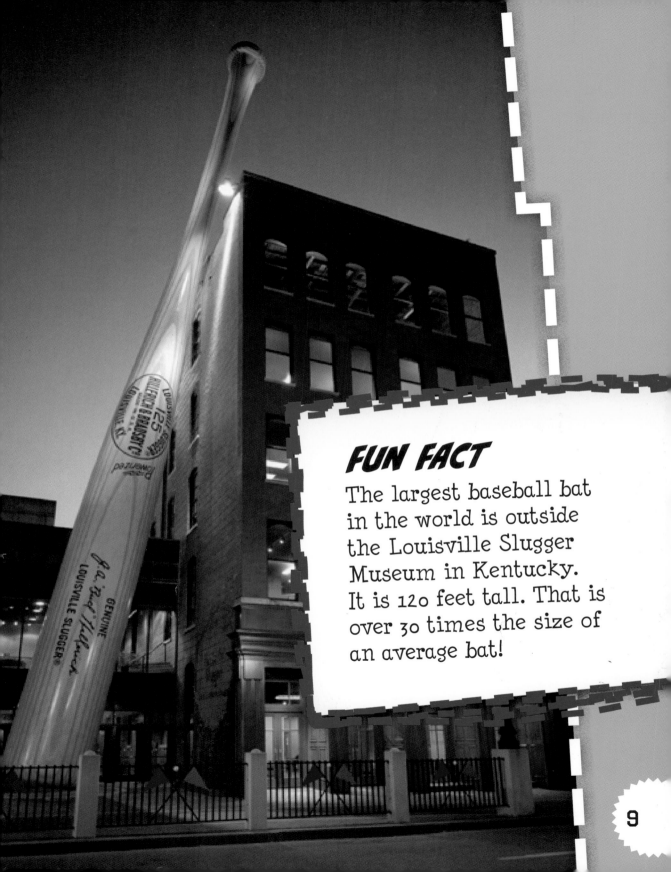

## FUN FACT

The largest baseball bat in the world is outside the Louisville Slugger Museum in Kentucky. It is 120 feet tall. That is over 30 times the size of an average bat!

9

# Amazing Achievements

Aroldis Chapman holds the record for the fastest-ever pitch. In 2010, he threw the ball at an astonishing 105.1 miles (169.1 kilometers) per hour!

In 2004, Ichiro Suzuki broke a long-standing record for the number of hits in a season. He had 262 hits.

DID YOU KNOW?

The previous record of 257 hits had lasted for 84 years!

# Huge Crowds

The record for the highest **attendance** at a baseball game is 115,300 people. This huge crowd watched the LA Dodgers play the Boston Red Sox in 2008. They filled the Los Angeles Coliseum.

12

## DID YOU KNOW?

The oldest ballpark in the United States is Rickwood Field, in Birmingham, Alabama. It was built in 1910.

13

# A-Rod and Prince Albert

Baseball stars earn a lot of money to play the sport they love. Alex Rodriguez, nicknamed "A-Rod," plays for the New York Yankees. He is paid $32 million a year!

14

**DID YOU KNOW?**

In 2012, Japanese pitcher Yu Darvish joined the MLB from the NPB (see page 5). He is paid $10 million a year.

Albert Pujols, nicknamed "Prince Albert," will be paid $250 million over the next 10 years.

15

# Tallest and Shortest

The tallest player to have played in Major League Baseball history is Jon Rauch. He is 6 feet 11 inches tall.

The shortest player to ever play was only 3 feet 7 inches tall. His name was Eddie Gaedel, and he only played one game in his Major League career.

### FUN FACT

Eddie Gaedel's jersey is in the Baseball Hall of Fame. It has the number 1/8 on it!

17

# Curse of the Bambino

The Red Sox managed to break the curse when they won in 2004.

Baseball fans believe that a **curse** began when Babe Ruth left the Boston Red Sox to play for the New York Yankees in 1919. After Ruth left, the Red Sox did not win a World Series for 86 years!

**FUN FACT**

A fan's pet goat was refused entry to the Wrigley Field ballpark during the 1945 World Series. The man cursed the team, and the Cubs have not competed in a World Series since!

WRIGLEY FIELD HOME OF CHICAGO CUBS

TICKETS ON SALE WWW.CUBS.COM

19

# Chicken Man

Many baseball players are **superstitious**. Former **third baseman** Wade Boggs used to eat a chicken before every game he played to bring him luck.

Wade ate so many chickens that he was given the nickname "Chicken Man"!

20

## FUN FACT

Famous **pitcher** Turk Wendell would brush his teeth between innings for good luck. He also jumped high over the **baseline** after pitching.

21

# Great Catch

Baseball fans love the chance to get involved in a game. Many fans take a mitt with them when they go to watch games. If a ball is hit into the stands, they try to catch it!

## FUN FACT

By March 2012, baseball fan Zack Hample had caught or collected an amazing 5,819 balls at 48 different stadiums!

# Great Players

Henry "Hank" Aaron is one of the all-time great players in baseball. He held the record for the most **home runs** in baseball history for over 30 years. Aaron scored an amazing 755 home runs during his career.

## DID YOU KNOW?

One of the most famous and successful baseball players is Derek Jeter. He has helped the New York Yankees to win five World Series titles.

25

**FIND OUT**
How did Jackie Robinson change baseball forever in 1947?

Jackie Robinson is a baseball legend. He played baseball in the 1940s and 1950s. His jersey number, 42, is worn by MLB players each year on Jackie Robinson Day as a tribute.

## DID YOU KNOW?

The record for the longest hitting streak in baseball history is held by Joe DiMaggio. He managed to get a hit in 56 games in a row.

27

# Quiz

Are you a superfan or a couch potato? Decide whether the statements below are true or false. Then look at the answers on page 31 and check your score on the fanometer.

**1** The New York Yankees have won the most World Series.

**2** Albert Pujols' nickname is "King Albert."

**3** The first ever World Series took place in 1903.

**TOP TIP**
Some of the answers can be found in this book, but you may have to find some yourself.

**4** Derek Jeter has helped the New York Yankees to win three World Series.

**5** Babe Ruth hit over 700 **home runs** in his career.

**6** The fastest pitch ever recorded was 100 miles (161 kilometers) per hour.

# FANOMETER

fair-weather fan

couch potato

superfan

1  2  3  4  5  6

29

# Glossary

**attendance** number of people who are at an event to see it

**Baseball Hall of Fame** museum in Cooperstown, New York, full of baseball items, books, and photographs

**baseline** line that marks the edge of the playing area

**curse** call or prayer for something bad to happen

**home run** when the ball is hit out of the playing area, and the player runs around all of the bases

**legendary** very famous

**pitcher** position on the field. The pitcher throws the baseball towards the batter.

**superstition** belief that is not based on reason, or evidence

**third baseman** fielding position

**traditional** something that has existed or been done for a long time

**winning margin** amount that a team or player wins by

# Find Out More

## Books

Doeden, Matt. *The Greatest Baseball Records* (Sports Records). Mankato, Minn.: Capstone Press, 2009.

LeBoutillier, Nate. *The Best of Everything Baseball Book*, Mankato, Minn.: Capstone Press, 2011.

## Websites

Facthound offers a safe, fun way to find Internet sites related to this book. All of the sites on Facthound have been researched by our staff.

Here's all you do:

Visit www.facthound.com

Type in this code: 9781410951076

## Quiz answers

1) True. The New York Yankees have won the World Series 27 times.
2) False. His nickname is "Prince Albert" (see page 15).
3) True. Boston won the first ever World Series in 1903.
4) False. Jeter has won the World Series five times with the New York Yankees (see page 25).
5) True (see page 8).
6) False. The fastest pitch ever recorded was 105.1 miles (169.1 kilometers) per hour (see page 10).

# Glossary